Give Yourself
Permission

LaTraci Aldridge

ISBN:

Give Yourself Permission

Copyright © 2024 by LaTraci Aldridge

For permission requests, please contact the author via email at laldridge22@gmail.com.

Proudly self-published through Divine Legacy Publishing, www.divinelegacypublishing.com

Introduction

Where do I begin? The idea for this book came to me when I was dealing with my husband's medical issues. Let's just say it was just a really tough and uncertain time, and it's still hard to believe that we went through that time. I don't know if this book is a self-help book or just me getting all the words inside me out on paper...maybe a little of both. Sit back and follow me on this journey and maybe something along the way will help you on your journey.

First, I want to give you background on the medical issues my family faced. Below is a blog I wrote about it.

In Sickness and in Health

Today, I'm writing about marriage. I guess you could say that's what it's about. As you can see, the title I chose for this blog is a line in most people's vows when they repeat after the officiant/pastor. *In sickness and in health.* So, most of us have said these words, and I'm sure especially in that moment we meant it. One, because in that moment you are bursting with love because you're marrying the love of your life. Two, because who truly thinks that one day the "in sickness" part of those vows would be knocking at your door? Especially when two people are young and pretty much healthy. So, we repeat those words with conviction, and we mean them.

In sickness and in health

My husband and I have been married since 2006. Whew chile, that was a long time ago. I don't feel like I'm old enough to have been married that long, but yet here we are. Of course, during that time, we have had our share of ups and downs, joys and pains, and wins and losses. It hasn't always been easy or a love fest. And anyone that tells you that marriage is always a love fest and roses is full of shit. Now, that's not to say that the majority of the time it can't be that way, but I'm a realist and do my best to keep it real with myself and others. My favorite thing to say about marriage is if you don't want to kick him in the throat every once in a while, it isn't real. But then there are those other times he makes you wanna…(Use your imagination here and yes it should be in the gutter LOL). Over the years we have had to face sickness but never anything too serious or life threatening. He has had to watch and help me through two c-sections and two other surgeries to have cysts removed that thankfully weren't cancerous. I've been right there when he started having issues with his blood pressure

2

and then thyroid issues. We made it through all of those things and more. And then…

In sickness and in health.

Sickness decided it wanted to come tap on our door June 10th. Really before that day, but we just didn't know it. For a few days, my husband had been complaining of having a really bad headache along with some other things. I told him that he should probably go to the doctor that Sunday. He didn't. He started to feel better, but a few days later things changed.

June 10th started out just like any other day. He got up and went to work. I got up and went to work. Work for me, at the time, was on 1000. I was in the midst of graduation season, so my stress level was on 1000. I was trying to figure out which one of my 500 kids were graduating and which ones weren't and coordinating graduation at a place that we normally didn't do graduation and I had no desire to do ever again (that's a story for another day, LOL).

June 10th was graduation rehearsal day. As I was headed downtown to rehearsal, I called to check in with my husband because he called earlier saying he wasn't feeling great, had been sweating really bad, and was nauseous. By this time, he decided he was going back to the doctor. He went the day before and they pretty much felt everything was fine. With how the next few days transpired, I'm not really sure how they determined that. But anyways, as I headed downtown, my husband was headed to the doctor. Just as I was getting ready to start rehearsal, my phone rings...unknown number. I didn't answer. I didn't have the time; I was really busy. They could leave a message, and it was probably one of those car warranty people. It rang again, but again I didn't answer. Then my husband's mom called. Now I knew something wasn't right, but I wasn't sure what. I answered and she told me my husband called her and said he wanted everybody at the hospital. She had no clue what was going on just that he was really emotional. I called back the number that kept calling. It was the emergency room.

In sickness and in health.

I was transferred to my husband's room. He was emotionally a mess, but he told me they had found bleeding on his brain. At this point, I was on the floor in the middle of a hallway of a convention center. I heard what he said, but I couldn't fully comprehend exactly what he was telling me. Then he let me talk to the doctor. I asked questions, but what I truly wanted and needed to ask was, "Is my husband about to die?" I don't know a whole lot about brain bleeds, but what I did know was that it wasn't good. Once I started thinking about what the doctor told me and some of the symptoms my husband had over the past few days, I started to get a feeling of de ja vu and not a good one. See, when my daddy died it all started with a headache and him sweating profusely and it was due to a brain aneurysm, but I told myself that's not what this was and had to pray to keep those thoughts at bay.

At this time, we still didn't know all of what was going on, only that my husband needed to transport to a hospital downtown where they had a neurology department. I mustered up enough strength to tell my co-worker what was going on and that I was checked out. She immediately took over with no problem.

Just a sidebar here - get you some co-workers who will hold you down when it all hits the fan, even personally. I couldn't ask for a better team to work with.

My co-worker told me to just go she had it. I didn't leave though, because he was supposed to be transported downtown at some point. I didn't want to head towards him if he was coming to where I was. So, I waited, and another co-worker sat with me to make sure I was okay. At that point, I started texting my support team, the ones I knew would hold me down when I needed it, and let them know something was going on with my husband. And, just like a true support team, they didn't hesitate to offer help with whatever I needed. I waited at the convention center for two hours before I drove to the hospital he was supposed to be transported to, and I waited there for at least an hour. He still hadn't been transported. I called the ER where he was to see how much longer his transport would take. They could only tell me they were waiting on a bed and that could be in the next five minutes or five hours. After that I just went to him.

In sickness and in health.

We spent the night in the ER because a bed never became available. As much as this annoyed me, there was also a part of me that took that to mean he wasn't in danger or getting worse or things weren't as bad as I may have imagined. Because, in my mind, if he was in a life-threatening situation they wouldn't just leave him sitting in an ER room all night. As least that was what I was hoping.

He didn't get transported downtown until the next day around noon. Once he got there and we start talking with the doctors, we learned that my husband had

5

suffered a stroke. I was shocked. He was shocked. In a way, the doctors were shocked. The doctors were shocked at the number of days he was experiencing symptoms but yet he was doing much better than one may have expected. He was still able to talk. He hadn't lost mobility. He still had a headache but, given the situation, that wasn't surprising.

My husband stayed in the hospital for a few days with a plan to go see a neurologist soon and begin some new medicine to manage his blood pressure. Okay, cool. We had a plan. I could work with a plan. I found a neurologist that was connected to the hospital he was in so we could get started on figuring out how he ended up having a stroke and what needed to be done to prevent it from happening again. One of the first things his neurologist noticed was the area of his brain bleed. Where it was located was not the normal location when a brain bleed was due to high blood pressure. He let us know that didn't mean that wasn't the cause, but it was not likely. The doctor scheduled an angiogram so we could hopefully get to the bottom of it. My husband hated the thought. Meanwhile, I was like get over that; we need to know what's going on because the alternative I can't deal with. The procedure was set for a week and half later.

In sickness and in health.

If you know me, you know I'm not a morning person. Of course, on the day of his procedure, we had to be at the hospital before the butt crack of dawn. Thankfully, we made on time. The procedure was supposed to take place at 7:30am and we should have been done and headed home by noon. First, they didn't see his name. Then, they see that he was an add-on so it may take longer. Unfortunately, all this did was increase his anxiety about the procedure even more. What should have taken place at 7:30am didn't take place until almost 1pm.

Once he was done and back in recovery, they called to let me know and told me they would call me again when he was moved to the second recovery room where I could come back. A few hours later his doctor came out to tell me that he started to notice that my husband was losing some mobility on his right side, so he wanted him to stay overnight for observation just to make sure everything was okay. I said okay while trying to keep my anxiety and worry at bay, then I was able to go see him.

He was awake and talking but was really groggy and kind of hard to understand. We sat and talked for a bit, and I let him know I needed to run to the store since we were staying the night. Of course, I wasn't prepared for this since it was supposed to be an in and out procedure. I ran to the store to get a few things and something to eat. Once I got back, the nurse lets me know they had a room ready for him so I needed to wait in the lobby until they moved him.

Not much longer after that, his doctor came back out. He told my husband was not doing good, and he may have a blood clot, so the doctor needed to go back in and clear it. I signed some paperwork but there was a part of me that wanted to scream "Y'all already went in him today and look how that is turning out!" But I know if it was, in fact, a clot, it needed to be cleared. A few hours later, the doctor came back out to let me know there was some good news. There was no clot when he went in. However, he may have suffered another stroke or possibly a seizure. Now he was being admitted to the ICU.

In sickness and in health.

Around midnight he was finally in an ICU room, and I got to see him. He was out of it and couldn't talk. I couldn't stay because it was the ICU. so I left, but I was back the next morning looking for answers. His doctors (because at this point it was a team of doctors) tried to get answers, but they kept coming up empty handed. No knew why he had the initial stroke. Blood pressure was fine. He'd been taking his meds. Thyroid issue was under control. At that point, all we knew was my husband wasn't doing well. He had lost mobility on his right side. He wasn't able to speak, and he ended up having to be put on a ventilator. A ventilator was something I knew very little about, but what I did know was that those didn't get used unless it was serious.

Thankfully, the nurses kept my anxiety at bay by letting me know there were multiple reasons people were put on ventilators and that this was just a temporary measure for him. By this time, his doctors had determined that he would need rehab, but they weren't sure for how long and what would be needed. They had a place in Atlanta that was state of the art for patients like my husband. As I was hearing all of this, I was looking at my husband who appeared to be helpless, and I just wanted to know how and why.

The doctors were just as baffled by everything that had taken place as I was. Everything that my husband has experienced had all been 1 in a 100 chance of happening. Not only had all of that baffled them, but his progress had been shocking to them. I was pretty sure if someone read his medical files and saw the scans of what was going on, they would have expected this to end or be another way.

My husband was now on day eight of being in the ICU but had made progress every day. Although he still couldn't speak, he had been able to communicate more with assistance. I had gotten the chance to see him smile or laugh once or twice. On my birthday, I walked in and asked him if he knew what the day was. He nodded yes. Then I asked if he wanted me to dance since it was my birthday. He told me no, but then he laughed. He also asked me where I parked my car because he was ready to go. I didn't know what the next few days or weeks look like for us, but I would be there in sickness and in health.

My husband was in ICU for two weeks. During this time, he was on a ventilator and had a feeding tube put in. He couldn't talk. He couldn't walk or move his arms much higher than an inch or so. There were times when he had to be restrained because he kept trying to pull out the various cords he was connected to. He hated those restraints. Usually, when he was motioning for something it was to see if they would loosen up the restraints or remove them. During those two weeks, we did a lot of wait and see. The plus side was that although during the first few days we were just hit with bad news, as time progressed that changed. He wasn't at a point that we could go home, but he also wasn't getting worse and given the situation that was all we could ask for.

Everything that was a less than 1% chance of happening happened. Ninety-nine percent of the time, angiograms happen without any issues. Most times, the procedure doesn't cause another stroke. But all of that happened with my husband. I told him he was trying to be a clinical case study. His neurologist recommended that my husband be transferred to a rehabilitation center as soon as he was medically able to be moved. His suggestion was a place in Atlanta called the Shepherd Center. Me being me I go talk to my BFF, Google, to see what this place was about and if we should really be considering moving my husband there to recover. And then came all of the questions. I'm an overthinker and over analyzer, so I had to think about every possible outcome and setback that could come with this decision. One of the biggest questions I had was "What is this going to cost?" Then, I had to think about how he was going to get there because he was still on a ventilator and had a feeding tube, so me driving him wasn't going to be an option. We knew what needed to happen, but how was it going to happen?

And then the insurance battle began. We all know our health care system is not in the best shape, but you truly never know just how much it needs an overhaul until you are in a situation where you are truly leaning on your insurance company to come through. The doctors at the hospital were truly some MVPs. They said my husband was a prime candidate for the Shepherd Center and that's where he needed to be. Because it was what they recommended, that is what me, his mom, and his sister set out to make happen no matter what. The first time the doctors went to the insurance company to request coverage for Shepherd Center, the insurance company said no.

Thankfully we had some doctors who truly cared and weren't going to just push us off to whatever insurance agreed to. They went head-to-head with the insurance company until they did what was right. Although there are rehabilitation hospitals in Memphis, there weren't any that offered rehabilitation services as extensive and intensive as the Shepherd Center. The doctors were able to get the insurance company to agree to cover my husband being treated at the Shepherd Center. Just as we were happy to overcome this hurdle, the insurance company threw another one at us. Getting my husband to the Shepherd Center. As I mentioned earlier, he was still on a ventilator and had a feeding tube so going by car wasn't happening.

The doctors went back to work fighting for us, but this time the insurance company wouldn't budge. This led me to believe that they only approved the coverage for the Shepherd Center with the hopes that we wouldn't be able to or wouldn't find a way to get him there. I can't confirm this, but they knew the condition he was in and knew the only way he would be able to be transported would be by ambulance or medical airplane. The other MVPs in the story are our family and friends because they wouldn't let an insurance hurdle stop us from getting my husband the care he needed. We were able to get an ambulance transport for him. The next morning at 7am he was headed to Atlanta, and I was right behind him.

Once everything was confirmed that he was heading to Shepherd Center, it was on me to get everything else in order, which wasn't an easy task. It wasn't easy because the only thing we knew was the date he was heading to Atlanta, but we had no idea how long he would be there. When you go on a vacation, you know how long you will be gone, how much to pack, and what all you need to pack. That night when I got ready to leave the hospital, I asked him what specific things he wanted me to bring. Although he still couldn't talk, he could mouth words which I sometimes couldn't make out or he would type on my laptop which was still very difficult for him to do. There was even one day he typed out "Where is your car?" because he wanted me to take him home. Of course, that wasn't happening. The main thing he asked for was his shoes. If you know him, you know nothing, not even a stroke, will stop him from getting his shoes.

Before I left for the night, the hospital offered to let our boys come up to see my husband since they hadn't seen him in two weeks even though it was against the hospital COVID and ICU rules. For that I was grateful. We called them on Facetime to check in and just seeing them on the phone was too much for him and couldn't handle them coming in to see him in the state he was in. My oldest, whose personality is much like his dad's, couldn't really handle it either and didn't stay on the phone that long. They were able to say a few words to him before I left to get our things together for our stay in Atlanta.

As I started to think about what you pack for a stay in a rehabilitation center for an undetermined amount time, there was a part of me that was calm. A big part of that had to do with our friends and family who allowed us to make this journey without the worry of a lot of things. When this all started, I went back and forth about setting up a GoFundMe account. I am that one who struggles with asking for help even when I may be on the verge of drowning. In true counselor fashion, it may not be hard to help others but asking for help ourselves can sometimes be a struggle. Once I knew we would have to be in Atlanta for undetermined amount of time, I set up the account. Between the GoFundMe, family, and friends I was able to survive while in Atlanta and not worry about anything financially speaking.

Even before the GoFundMe account was setup, some of the best line sisters one could have sent me flowers, a card, and two gift cards I could use to eat, get gas, or whatever else I would need while in Atlanta. And my in-laws where right behind them in helping us getting whatever we needed. With most of my worries behind me, we made the trip to Atlanta. Me in my car and him in the ambulance, which didn't really allow for me to check in. I did the next best thing I could and cranked up my "Road to Recovery" playlist, let the stress leave my body, and let the music push me forward. Just like dancing, music allows me to lose myself and forget everything just for a moment.

That playlist became my go to when I needed a re-up on staying positive. One song in particular I played every single morning when I would head to the hospital and every time I left the hospital when he was still in Memphis. The song was "Anything for You" by Ledisi. It was just something about that song that kept pulling me into him and had me recalling why I needed him to get better. The lyrics just expressed everything I was feeling while going through this. One part that stuck out was the second verse. It says:

"Time, don't wanna waste no more time

On broken pieces from the past

We have now, nothing's better than right now

I'm committed to you, and you are to me"

With everything we were dealing with, it made every argument, disagreement, disappointment or whatever seem so small and pointless. None of that mattered in these moments. I just wanted him back and would do anything to have that, and that meant heading to Atlanta and not really thinking about what that meant for work or anything else at the time. Because if he was going to Atlanta, that's where I was going and for however long he needed to be there.

I got to the Shepherd Center before he did, and I took care of the paperwork while we waited for him to arrive.

Although I hated that we even had to go through this, I was glad to have gone through it with the wonderful people at the Shepherd Center. The Shepherd Center was everything I was told it would be and more. Not only did they take care of my husband, but me as well. I was able to stay on campus in my own apartment style room the entire time my husband was there. It wasn't luxurious by anyone's measure, but it was also one less thing I had to worry about. When my husband arrived, he was immediately taken to his ICU room at Shepherd and checked out. He still had not been waned off the ventilator for at least 24 hours before leaving Memphis, so he had to be admitted to ICU at Shepherd. Thankfully, the hospital in Memphis took him off the vent before heading to Atlanta and he would be off it completely after arriving to Shepherd. One milestone completed towards recovery.

The first day was really just getting acclimated to the facility and getting familiar with my/our temporary home. The facility had on site housing that allowed me to be just seconds away from him. The facility was state of the art and the work that was done there was beyond phenomenal. The nurses, PTs, RTs, and every staff member there were very welcoming and I cannot thank them enough being part of my husband's journey to recovery. When he first arrived, he couldn't talk, walk, eat, or drink anything. Although he no longer was on the ventilator, he still had a trach, a feeding tube, and had to use a wheelchair. The first few days were full of paperwork and meeting various people on his medical team. He had doctors and specialists for everything. Some of the specialists I had never heard of.

Since we arrived on a Friday, he had a very light schedule and most of the day was spent in his room.

Once Monday came, it was go-time. He had a full day Monday- Friday that started around 7am with him getting bathed. This was not your "Coming to America, your royal penis is clean your highness" type of bath. He hated it, and me being the true Memphian that I am, I clowned him for this. Some of you may be thinking that was just cruel given the situation, but if you're a Memphian you know checkin' a loved one is a way to show affection. Since I knew we were out of the woods as far as him being on the mend, it was only right, and who knew how long I would be able to say whatever I needed to say on him without him being able to say anything back. So, I had to take advantage of this time.

Since his days were full of various therapy sessions, I spent most days sitting in the family lounge of the facility working. Yeah, I was still working in the midst of my world being turned upside down. As much as I am an advocate for work-life balance, having that also helped me. Otherwise, I would have been just sitting in the apartment I was staying in or spending unnecessary money to make the time pass. I'm a high school counselor and when everything happened with my husband it was also the year of COVID, and we were one of the many school districts that pushed the start of the school year back which meant that we would also be getting out later in the year. That meant a short, very short, summer break. Two weeks to be exact. Summertime was also when we prepared for the next year by making sure schedules were in order and transcripts were updated. Therefore, not being at work and not doing what I could from Atlanta would mean walking back into a bigger hot mess than what I would normally be walking to in the beginning of the year. As a senior counselor, it's a toss up on if the beginning of the year or the end of the year (will you or won't you graduate) is the worse part of the year. Additionally, having a semi-set schedule allowed me to have some normalcy in the midst of nothing being normal.

I stepped into my temporary new normal. Get up, eat, work, eat lunch, work a little more, then head to his room. Sometimes I would get to his room and he would still be in therapy and other times he would be sitting in the bed or in his wheelchair. Every time I would walk in his room and he was in there, he would mouth "I'm ready to go home." Every single time without fail. He wanted to get better. Back to walking. Back to talking. But more than anything he wanted to go home. By this time, it had been over two weeks since he was at home or slept in his own bed. Most days he was very tired because they pushed him.

One of the reasons his doctors recommended the Shepherd Center was because they knew just how much care he would receive and what was needed for someone in his position. If we had of stayed at a facility in Memphis, he would have received care but not at the rate and intensity that he did at Shepherd. At home, he would have gotten therapy maybe three times a day or three times a week. At Shepherd he received speech therapy, physical therapy, recreation therapy, and occupational therapy five days a week and sometimes six days. On some occasions, he would have the same type of therapy twice in a day. Their goal was to get him as close to what he used to be as they could before they sent him home to finish recovering.

During the first week, we had a meeting with the lead doctor, a Physical Medicine and Rehabilitation physician or PMR. This was a type of doctor I had never heard of. During the meeting, we went over my husband's scans from Memphis and the scans they did when he first got to Atlanta. They were able to show us where his strokes took place in his brain. The first stroke took place in on his left side towards the temporal lobe. The second stroke took place more towards his cerebellum and brain stem in his pons. These areas are responsible for balance, breathing, and swallowing just to name a few things. This explained why he had the deficits he had, but it still didn't tell us why he had the strokes to begin with. We were reminded again that 20% of people who have strokes will never know exactly why they had a stroke. For me, that made it a little harder to deal with. I've already gone through watching my husband endure something so unexpected that we could have never prepared for, so if they couldn't tell us why the strokes happened how could he do work to prevent another one? I understood that he might not be able to 100% prevent another stroke, but at least knowing why so we can pinpoint that could increase his chances of preventing it. Unfortunately, no matter how many scans they ran, they couldn't tell us the why. They hoped that when we returned home, his doctor could perform more tests or send him to other specialists to try to determine the cause. We could only hope that would get us answers one day.

The rest of the week his therapy sessions allowed all of the specialists to determine a baseline for where he was. When we arrived, he still had a trachea and the feeding tube. He wasn't able to walk on his own, talk, eat, or write. He was able to mouth some words and point to letters on a keyboard or notepad with letters. In some cases, I was able to understand what he was trying to say and others I wasn't, which was frustrating for both of us. I'm sure more for him than me.

As they were working with him on learning to walk and talk again, they were also training me on how to assist him because we didn't know how long he would be there and what his progress would be when he left, so I needed to be aware of how to assist him, if needed. I was taught how to use the medical belt to hold him as he tried to walk. The first days were really hard, and the PTs had to physically move his legs to show him and his body how to walk again. The ST worked with him on swallowing and learning to mouth his words more. The OT worked with him on daily life tasks like taking a bath and moving small objects to help with his gross motor skills. After they were able to determine where he was, we were informed that his tentative discharge date would be August 11th. Just three days before his birthday.

With a discharge date on the table, he put in the work, but he was ready to go home every step of the way. Every single time I came to his room, he would say hello by saying "I'm ready to go home." EVERY SINGLE TIME! And I would just say "Well hello to you, too." And this was the case even before he was able to talk again. Of course, the main reason he was ready to go because it had been weeks since he had been home and in his own bed. Beyond that, he was ready to go because he also had a roommate. Unfortunately, he wasn't able to have a private room, but he did have a privacy liner that allowed for some privacy. If you know my husband, he is not the "never met a stranger" kind of guy. Now, the roommate, on the other hand, was a different story. His roommate would try to hold conversations with him, and he would usually respond with a head nod or very little feedback. He was there for treatment and nothing more.

Although this time was trying for us, there were some moments that you just couldn't help but laugh. One of those times was when another patient came into their room and became very adamant that my husband was his nephew and he wanted to come talk to him. While that patient was saying he knew my husband was his nephew, his roommate proceeded to tell the other patient to "Come on in and take a rest." At this point, I was in my chair laughing because what else do you do. The staff was able to come get the other patient out the room but not before he locked his wheelchair so they couldn't pull him out the room and demanded again "I know my nephew." Needless to say, my husband was ready to go home even more.

In spite of everything, we also made time to make the best of the situation. When I would come to his room in the afternoons, and we would usually find something on Netflix to watch if we couldn't find anything on the hospital TV to watch. Since Netflix was on my laptop, that meant I had to sit in the bed with him for us to both be able to see it. Normally this wouldn't be an issue, but this was a twin size hospital bed with a camera above our heads, so I wasn't really feeling it most of the time. And you can't forget the nurses, respiratory therapists, the techs, and whoever else needed to come in what felt like every 15 minutes and do what they needed to do. I would try to use them as my way of escaping the twin bed, but every time they failed me by saying "Oh no you're fine. No need to get up. That's so sweet." I would try to plead with my eyes that no I wasn't fine, my back is hurting, but they never read my eyes. However, these were also the moments we enjoyed. This allowed us time together that had we been at home we wouldn't have gotten. And definitely not just by ourselves. We weren't completely by ourselves, but you know what I mean.

As the weeks went by, he became stronger. He was able to take steps with assistance. He was able to finally eat real food. The first day he had real food you would have thought he was eating the finest food known to man. It was just some hospital fried chicken, but when you haven't been able to have real food in over a month anything is better than what you have had. He was loving it and ate it all and it had me cracking up watching him eat. He also started to speak again. Although he still had the trach in, they were able to put a speaking valve over the trach hole, and not even 10 minutes after he was able to talk again, I was hoping he would hush. In true old married life fashion. I may have even threatened to take his speaking valve out a time or two. Although he still wouldn't talk to the staff. They had no idea he was able to speak until I came in one day, busted him out, and let them know that he could now talk.

The next few weeks were just more of the same. Me working and getting prepped for the school year and him working to get better. There were a few things they wanted to take place before his potential discharge date of August 11th which if he didn't achieve would mean possibly staying longer. For one, they wanted him to be able to get rid of his secretions on his own so his trach could be taken out. Up until that point, he would have to be manually suctioned out with a machine. This also limited him to where he could go in the facility. The facility had other areas that would allow him to get out of his room, but we had to be escorted by a tech in case something medically happened while he was away from the unit. For me to be able to take him off the floor, I had to be cleared to lift him from his wheelchair to his bed

20

and to be able clear out his trach should he need to clear his lungs. This was needed because if he didn't, he ran the risk of getting pneumonia again which he did get before we left Memphis. Although I had watched several nurses suction him out over these weeks, me having to do it was a different ball game. To suction him out I had to glove up and make sure I didn't touch the end of the tube that would be going down his throat. Then I had to stretch the tube and stick it down the hole where the trach was. Then, the part he really hated, I had to turn on the compressor which would suck up any loose mucus in his lungs. He hated it because it would also force him to cough which hurt. I was cleared to do it so that meant I could take him off the unit by myself.

With this new freedom, he was able to eat lunch in the cafeteria and go to the garden where he could visit with family through a gate. Since we were still knee deep in the pandemic, the facility had a very strict visitation policy. He was only allowed to have two people visit his room the entire time he was there. That was me and his mom. Anyone else would have to see him outside through a gate and only when a tech was free to take him. But once I was cleared with everything, I was able to take him, and I finished everything just in time for the kids visit. He hadn't seen the kids since June 28th when he went for his procedure. August 2nd was the next time he would see them. Our family came and brought them for us to see them, because I had only seen them a few times since June 28th myself. It was hard for the boys because although they were staying with me on the facility campus, they still couldn't go see him. We coordinated a time after all of his therapy that they would meet us at the gate while I brought him down.

Normally, he would let me push him or he would push himself. This time was different. As soon as he saw their faces, he rolled faster than I have ever seen him roll in his chair. Honestly, I was afraid he was going to roll out the chair he was going so fast. He even bypassed the caution tape they had by the gate for visitations to keep people at a distance. It was a tender and hard moment all at the same time. But since he bypassed the caution tape, we had a visitor: security. They saw us on camera and told us we had to move back. Part of me got it but the part of me that knew it had been a month since they'd seen each other wanted to scream let us have this moment. I mean it was limited already. He was talking to them through a gate. We moved back. Mainly because security wasn't leaving until we did. I think seeing them gave him the last push he needed to make it the last two weeks. Because he was so down all the time, I was worried it would affect his progress.

As a therapist, I know how important a positive mindset can be especially when you are trying to work towards something. I did my best to try to keep him uplifted throughout this, but it was just hard. He was not happy with his situation, and the memory of how he used to be was a constant reminder that he wasn't the same. At times, he seemed to only focus on that and nothing else. It was the reason why he always greeted me with "I'm ready to go home." Not only did I try to get him to keep a positive attitude, but there was also a weekend desk nurse who did. She was from Mississippi and so we hit it off because it's a southern thing. One day we got him out the room a little bit and she told him she would have some 8Ball and MJG when he came back. Even if only for a few moments, he had a smile on his face.

The last few weeks were just making sure he would be strong enough to head home. They wanted to make sure we had everything we needed to continue his progress once we returned. He did have the option to step down to their outpatient care but of course he wanted no parts of that because he wanted to get home. Me too. The first day out of the hospital, I decided to get a hotel and stay one night because I needed a day before we were bombarded with family and friends who wanted to check in. The first thing he wanted to do when he got out was go to the Nike factory. If you know my husband, nothing about this is surprising at all. So, I rolled my eyes and took him to Nike.

When we got home, he continued therapy. Mainly physical therapy since he was still in a wheelchair. He couldn't be by himself for the first thirty days, so he would stay at his mom's during the day, and I would pick him after work. This time, truthfully, may have been the most difficult part in this whole journey. For one, I think the realization of everything that happened to him seem to hit more when he got home and just knowing that he couldn't do some of simplest things he used to do was hard to deal with. Some days were really hard for both of us. They say when we struggle the people who are closest to us are the ones who get the brunt of our hurt. Some days I could be understanding of the situation because that's a difficult position to be in. And other days…well…that's when you have to give yourself permission . . .

LaTraci Aldridge

Give Yourself Permission . . .

To Lose Your Ish

I have already stated the idea for this book came while my husband was dealing with a medical crisis. In short, one day we were living life normal and then my husband called me from the hospital saying they had told him he had bleeding on his brain. World stop!

The next few days bring on a lot of uncertainty, and it was during these days that I went to my car one day and I lost it. In front of his family, talking with my friends and family, and talking to my kids I was okay. Well, I was not okay, but in true Traci fashion I had to be the one to hold it all together. So, in front of others,

I was as okay as one could be given the situation. But in the midst of all of this, I had to let it all out. I went to my car and I screamed. I cried. I questioned God about everything that was going on. I prayed that everything was going to be okay. In the midst of trying to hold it together in my car, I told myself give yourself permission to lose your ish. And that's exactly what I did in my car in that hospital parking garage. I let it all out. Everything I had been holding in.

Now you know how I got here.

What does "give yourself permission to lose your ish" really mean? I believe we live in a society where, women especially, scratch that... especially Black women... are expected to just take licks and keep on going with a smile on our faces. Who made that rule? Why are women expected to just always keep our stuff, the kids' stuff, the husband's stuff, and whoever else's stuff together? Who is going to keep us together, though?

One of the first things we must do is acknowledge that we are on the verge of losing it. I am the master of "I'm fine" or "I'm good." And we all know those phrases are Grade A BS! Well, at least 90% of the time they are. Why do we do that? Why say I'm fine when in reality you are 2.3 seconds from knocking your husband upside his head, telling your supervisor where they can go, or hopping in the car and never coming back? Don't eye me like you have never had these thoughts. Come on, tell the truth and shame the devil. What could just opening up and telling someone "I'm not okay" do for you? No one is saying you have you to bare your soul, but just acknowledge that you are at a place that is no longer okay.

What are you afraid of?

I'm sure one of the concerns is that people will judge you or tell your business. I know for those in the African American community, the latter is one of the biggest reasons we don't open up to others. So many of us have experienced or seen others deal with the hurt of someone telling their private thoughts to others. We must have discernment when deciding on who to let in. For some of us, we are too trusting, and others aren't trustworthy of anyone. There has to be some balance. If someone is trusting you with their "stuff" don't take advantage and don't tell it to others. For one, you wouldn't want it done to you. Second, you don't know just how hard it may have been for them to open up to you. You never know when the day may come that you may need to open up to someone.

How do you know you're at that point? What are your triggers? In some cases, the situation you're dealing with is the trigger. For example, me not knowing if my husband would live through his stroke or not was a major trigger for me. A trigger can be stress at work, at home, with a person, or with just life in general. If you can identify your triggers, you may be able to minimize them blowing up into bigger problems or increasing your stress levels, and you can better cope with the situation. Even though there are times that you may be able to cope with your stressors, there are some situations that in the moment can be too much. What do you do when it's too much?

Give yourself permission to lose it. We, especially Black women, are told to always keep it together. Maybe not in those exact words. It comes out as "You're so strong" or "I don't know how you do it all." It's the Black Women Superwoman Syndrome. Society has led us to feel like no matter what we are struggling with or

27

how much we are doing, we can just throw our cape on handle it. Then, we are praised for doing it which reinforces the superwoman syndrome. The truth is that we may be able to wear that cape in front of others and display a façade that we have it all together, but when we go home and take the cape off, we are struggling and broken. There are even times when we may try to let others know we're struggling and we're met with "You're strong, I know you got this" or "I know you can handle it" instead of being asked what we need or how we can be helped. And that's not to say we always know what we need.

What does losing your ish look like?

Well, that can look different for each one of us. For me, it was sitting in a hospital parking garage screaming, crying, and saying all of the things I hadn't said to anyone. I questioned why we were in this situation. I expressed how terrified I was at the possibility that I could lose my husband. I thought about what I would tell my kids. That part was honestly the hardest thing to think about and the part I tried to not to think about. I knew I could work through my own grief if it got to that point, but just how in the hell could I go home and tell my boys that their daddy was gone? Honestly, they didn't truly know it was a possibility. They just knew he was in the hospital, and he was sick. And not knowing how to tell them something like this is why I just kept praying that he would pull through. Not for me, but for them. I hadn't let those thoughts really be heard to others, and I had to get it out. That's what that moment in my car was for me.

One thing I talk about with my clients is releasing what's inside of them. We are all full of emotions and different situations can bring on more than the normal amount of emotions. We sometimes have a tendency to keep things bottled up inside, especially with the heavy stuff in life. When we hold our emotions in, we risk becoming a ticking time bomb. It starts off as holding in one thing in, then something else happens, and another thing, and before we know it, you have stifled so many emotions that the smallest thing can cause you to blow up. And that blow up can come out in a multitude of ways.

How can you release those emotions so it doesn't get to the point of you blowing up? Well, that depends on you! What works for one person may not work for you. My husband's second stroke happened just days before my birthday. We had plans to go out and listen to one of our favorite bands. We were talking about this before he went back for his procedure that altered our lives. With everything that was going on during that time, I had reached out to the promoter to see how I could get refund. Just hoping that my sad, but true, story would allow them to refund me even if they didn't normally do it. However, my sister (well his sister, but we don't do in-law) had other plans. She told me no we were still going on and that I needed to go.

Honestly, I really didn't have any desire to go anymore. I mean, I didn't know if I was going to get a call at any moment saying that my husband was getting worse or was no longer here. During this time, my life consisted of waking up, calling the hospital to check in, getting my coffee, going to the hospital to sit with my husband, going to grab lunch, coming back and sitting with my husband until visitation was over, grabbing some dinner, getting home and calling the hospital to check in one last time before going to sleep and then doing it all over again the next day. This was my life for two weeks, and because the hospital was still under COVID restrictions the number of visitors and how long we could visit were limited.

Needless to say, I was a ball full of emotions and going out and dancing the night away were the last things on my mind. Which, if you know me, is very out of the norm. Any other time dancing the night away to some good music was a form of therapy for me. Dancing is a way I release my emotions so what was holding me back from doing it now? I can tell you exactly what. First, emotionally I just wasn't sure I was up to it. Then, there was the worry of the hospital calling with a bad update and being out and not at home. And lastly there was some slight guilt about going out while my husband was at a hospital hooked up some several different cords and plugs, unable to move, talk, eat, and he was just alone. That was probably one of the biggest things that had me hesitant to still go out.

Just to bring you into my story more, let me tell you what it was like every single time I left the hospital. I would try to stay as late as I could, even past the visiting hours. Sometimes they put me out. But when I would leave, I would always tell him bye, hug him, tell him I would be back in the morning and every single time he would hold my hand and wouldn't let it go. He couldn't talk, but his eyes would plead with me not to leave, and every night it got harder and harder to leave. Do you realize how gut-wrenching that feeling is? And that just made the guilt of going out even higher.

But I went, and it was everything I needed in that moment. A little background on me. I'm a dancer. I have danced from a very young age all the way through to be on my school's dance team in college. During the event, the DJ called for all former majorettes and dancers to come to the floor. Of course, I had to oblige. Let's just say I was in my element. I got lost in the music. It is something so therapeutic for me when I get lost in music. For those few moments, my world isn't turning upside down. My husband wasn't fighting for his life. My boys weren't trying to figure out what exactly what was going with their dad whom they hadn't seen in three days. It was just me, some music, and old dance routines. Even in a room full of people, for those few moments it was just me and my therapeutic release. After that I was able to just be and enjoy the night and not worry about what was else what was going on.

One thing I had to realize during that time was that not being at the hospital 24/7 didn't take away from me wanting to be there for and with my husband. In addition, I had to come to the realization that in these moments there was nothing I could physically do to make my husband better or speed up his healing. On the other hand, I had to also take care of self. As a counselor, a healer, and a nurturer it can be very difficult, at times, to take care of self. We like to make sure others are good, but when asked are we good or need anything the response is normally, "No I'm good" when that may be the furthest thing from the truth.

Even in my moments of my release, I still had moments of worry and guilt throughout the night. There were times I would not be 100% engaged in the music or where I was because I was thinking about my husband. I would check my phone multiple times to make sure the hospital hadn't called. Even in my quest to leave my worries behind, I couldn't let them all go. And that is 100% okay. There is a part of me that felt that if people knew I was out having fun and cutting up like only I can, that someone would have something to say and think less of me. I'm one who usually doesn't worry or care about what others think, but I had also never been in a situation like this. So, it was different. I recall even taking a picture or two, but no one has ever seen them because I didn't need the judgement. That's not to say those I really cared about would judge me, but those feelings were still there. And on the ride home, I called the hospital to check in just like I had every night since he had been in the ICU.

Give Yourself Permission . . .
To Let It Go and Say F It!

Of course, with roses there are always thorns. Although, overall, we made the best of the situation at hand, the stress of everything eventually took its toll on both of us. For him, it was coping with being a different version of himself and feeling stuck with where he was physically, emotionally, and mentally. For me, it was trying to find the balance between being there for him but also taking care of myself in the process. Go figure, a counselor that struggled with self-care. Although I was starting to feel the effects of working, worrying about him, and being in his room anytime I wasn't working, I just kept going the way I was going. But I knew I couldn't continue it. So, I told him that I may not be coming up as much because I was getting worn out. I would still come but just not as much as I had been. He was not happy to hear that.

The counselor in me knew that his reasoning for not being happy was all due to his current state. Can you imagine one day living and doing just fine and you go in for a procedure and come out of it not being able to walk, talk, eat, or do anything on your own? Because I knew he was struggling with these feelings and emotions, I would put my own to the side for the most part. I'm a very self-aware person and can tell when I'm getting stressed way more than usual.

Being self-aware is something I try to work with my clients on. When you are self-aware, you can pick on your physical cues and changes in your body that come about when you are stressed. For me, I start to notice I'm more fatigued. I become more easily irritated. I can also to start to be more secluded and want to be alone more. I am the true definition of an extroverted introvert. I'm a very social person, but I also recognize when I'm low and need time to myself to recharge. I do my best to try to listen to my physical cues. One thing I have learned is that if you don't listen to your body when it's talking to you, you may be forced to listen to it when it sits you down.

I started to listen more to my body and my emotions. I knew being in his room all day when I wasn't working was wearing on me, so I didn't go straight to his room when his therapy ended or when I finished working. Instead, I would go back to my room, go shopping, or go find somewhere to sit down and eat instead of just eating at the hospital or picking up something and eating in my room. Needless to say, that didn't go over to well with him. For him, he was stuck and it did eat at him some that I wasn't stuck in just one location. Misery loves company. He, unfortunately, isn't one who tries to see the good in situations. Instead, he focuses on what's not going well. For me, who likes to try to see good in situations, that can be hard to be around all the time. I understood, as much as I could, why he felt the way he did. However, I knew I had to also take care of me, too. Otherwise, I couldn't be there for him.

One day I just had to take a break, and I told him I was going to come in later. Things were said and when it was all done, I decided to choose me regardless of what was going on or what he was dealing with. I left his room and didn't come back at all for a few days. I was tired, and I needed a break. I took it. I didn't really care how he felt about it or what anybody else felt about it. I was choosing me. This was my "F it" moment during this situation. I had to just say F it. Otherwise, I would have just continued to ignore my feelings and emotions and then where would I have been? Sometimes just saying F it is the best thing you can do. It may not seem like it in the moment, but it can be freeing and the path to new beginnings and better outcomes.

Sure, I could have just continued to go to his room or only stayed away for that one day, but I needed to take a step back and recharge. I also felt that I needed him to see that I needed a break too and this wasn't directly about him but me and my well-being. I did let him know that I was needing a break, but in his current state of mind it just wasn't registering. For him, he knew he was stuck and that I wasn't and that's all he could see. Me not coming by for a few days was my way of showing, not just telling, him that I needed a break, and I was going to choose me this time. Again, he wasn't too happy about it because that meant that he also wasn't getting any visitors. But, ultimately, I think it helped him to see that he wasn't the only going through this. He had said on a few occasions that he was the only having to deal with this. Which physically, yes that was true. However, that didn't mean I wasn't going through my own journey with this. I decided that in spite of everything else going on I chose me.

Society tells us that choosing us is selfish. That once you become a wife, a mom, an employee, or whatever that you no longer get to choose you. Well, society can kiss my tail. Choosing you isn't selfish but more about self-care. I tell my clients that sometimes you gotta be selfish, say F it to everybody else, and be okay with it being selfish. That part just may be the hardest part. We will choose us but then feel guilty about choosing us. Let the guilt go. If you never choose you, there may not be a you much longer to choose. What will it take to choose you sometimes? Like everything else in life, there has to be a balance. What's the worst thing that can happen if you choose yourself just once for a change?

You won't ever know unless you do it. Choosing yourself can look different depending on the person and the situation. In the situation with my husband, choosing me meant not waking up and going to his room. Instead, I woke up, grabbed breakfast, and then went to get my nails done. Nails that hadn't been done in over a month. In other situations, it could mean walking away from something or someone. For example, at my previous job, I recall applying for a different position that was more aligned with my degree. I had worked there for five years; why would I think they would not only hire someone else but someone that wasn't currently working for the company? But that is exactly what happened, and I found out while in a meeting that they were looking to extend an offer to someone. They hadn't even communicated that with me before the meeting. Thankfully, the meeting was virtual, so no one saw the disappointment in my face when they made that announcement.

Again, I decided that since they didn't choose me, I would choose me. While still sitting in the meeting, I looked up job openings in my local school district. One of the openings was for my high school alma mater. A place I would have loved to work. Not only did I graduate there, but I also did my internship there. Why not come full circle again? I applied on Friday, interviewed on Monday, and had the job by Monday evening. I put my notice in as soon as I knew all the paperwork was good. Choosing myself not only put me in a place I wanted to be, but it also increased my salary. That no from my current job was what pushed me. Truth be told, had that not happened I wouldn't have even looked for another job. In fact, the district office had reached out to me a few weeks prior to see if I would be interested interviewing for some principals, and I told them I was not looking for a job. Ha! Who would have thought that wouldn't have aged well?

That closed door allowed me to say F it and throw caution in the wind and it worked out in my favor. That may not always be the case, but you will never know what can happen unless you take the chance. I am not a big Steve Harvey advice fan, but there was one thing he talked about that I agree with. He said, "If you want to be successful, you have to jump, there's no way around it." Basically, you have to willing to just take a chance. You may not always land where you want, but you will land where you need to land. That may be hard to see when you are in the midst, but when you get on the other side of it – whew, what a beautiful feeling it is.

Now, to break down even more what F it means to me. It's more than just flipping the world and your situations off. It's deeper than that. To get to where you want to go in life you got dig deeper than surface level. Staying on the surface keeps you complacent and at times stuck.

F - Free yourself

U- Unleash your greatness

C- Clean your life

K- Keep your support close

I - Invest in yourself

T- Trust yourself

Free Yourself

When you let the perspectives and views that others have of you leave your line of thought, you start to be free. That's not to say you don't still think about what others say or think, but you don't let it dictate what you do. I'm a natural hair kind of girl and have been since around 2008 or 2009 (I don't 100% recall it wasn't a life altering/changing decision for me like most. I just did it). I wear my hair mainly in its natural state. One day I decided to straighten it. When I got to work my president saw me and said, "Oh, I like your hair. It's very professional." I think I froze in the hallway because I was that taken back by her statement. And yes, she was a white woman. Needless to say, I went home and washed my hair that same night. Not sure when hair became an indicator of how professional a person was.

I refused to let my hair dictate who I was as a person or an employee. My hair is most definitely a part of me, but it is not all that I am. There is so much more to me. To us. I believe society likes to put us in boxes and make us linear. We are complex beings that are multi-faceted. I can help you work through some of your trauma on a Monday then turn around it drop it like Meg on a Friday. I will still be me and still be the good therapist that I am. There are levels to me. We have to stop allowing people to keep us confined to the boxes they create for us. F them folks and free yourself.

To free yourself, you have to learn to fall in love with yourself. Have you ever just sat with yourself and studied who you are? If you haven't, you should. What are your likes? Dislikes? What's that thing you like to do when no one else is around? What have you been afraid to show the world because you were afraid of what others may think? Learning to love and accept yourself is one of the most beautiful things I have ever gone through. It was a gradual process, and it didn't just happen. I honestly don't know how or when it happened. I just know one day I was thinking about how much I have changed over the years and just thought "Girl, you are one dope chick."

Unleash Your Greatness

One thing I try to instill in my boys is that they come from greatness, so they can't help but be great. There is greatness in all of us. You just have to tap into it. Sometimes the only reason we haven't tapped into our greatness because of one person, and that person is YOU! Yes, you are holding you back. Stop that! There is too much greatness in you for you to just keep it bottled up. Let it out. Let the world see that greatness that's in you. Get out of your own way and let your light shine.

Ask yourself why you are in your own way. No really, ask yourself right now why. Most of us will say fear. That fear can be a number of things depending on what you are holding back from doing. It could be that you want to take that dive into the world of entrepreneurship, but that fear not being financial stable if you take that leap. It could be going back to school, but now you're older and you don't want others to focus on that. Or you fear you've been out of it too long so what's the point. Maybe it's something smaller and you just want to shoot your shot at that girl or guy you've been crushing on. As I mentioned earlier, you will ever know what could happen until you take that leap.

One way to overcome fear is knowledge. In life, there are many unknowns and that will sometimes keep us complacent. I'm one who likes to think about all of the possible outcomes when making decisions so no unknowns can create anxiety for me, but there is no way to ever know it all. I always joke it would be nice if God could just send me an email and let me know how and if things would work, life would be easier. But I don't think he has email. If he does and you have it, let me know. Although we can't know it all, we can arm ourselves with as much knowledge as possible to help ease our fears.

If you're wanting to be an entrepreneur, there are several people that have done this before you. Talk to current entrepreneurs to see what knowledge and advice they could give you. You can also look into getting a business coach. If you want to go back school, talk to current students, if possible, to see how you can incorporate school into what may already be a busy life. Some colleges will do mixers or meet and greets that will allow for this. You won't be the first or the last person that may be older or have started and stopped more than once or twice before. Going to college fresh out of high school with no real responsibilities is one thing but starting when you are six months pregnant or with two kids, a husband, and full-time job is a different beast. Both of those were my life story. It will be hard, but it can be done. Now, if you want to shoot your shot with the guy or girl, that's one you just gotta take. You can make sure there is a mutual interest there before shooting that shoot. But how many movies are about friends that have been hiding feelings from the other because they didn't think the other felt the same and then when they finally do, they wished they had of done it earlier.

Clean Your Life

We have all heard of spring cleaning. It's when you go through your closets and try to get rid of clothes you no longer wear (read: can't wear anymore). You do deeper cleaning that you may not normally get to do. But I'm not talking about that spring clean. Sometimes you have to spring clean your life. You have to take inventory of your life and see what needs to be "thrown out." That could mean limiting your time, interaction, and energy for certain people in your life. There may be some people in your life who are toxic or energy draining. How long will you allow them to suck life from you? What about those friends that you are always there to support but when it's time to support you they are nowhere to be found? If your friendship or other relationships seem to be one-sided, determine if it's time to move.

Other than spring cleaning certain people from your life, there may be some bad habits from your life. One thing I have been working on is trying to find more time for myself. If you're like me then you wear many hats. Sometimes it can feel like you don't know how many hats

41

you have. It's gotten to a point where if I don't put reminders in my phone with an alarm I will more than likely forget it.

As a counselor it can be hard at times to take time for myself because it's in my nature to care for others. I have learned over the years that I have to start taking time for myself more. One thing I started to do while I was working on my PhD was reading. It is how I unwind at the end of the day. Because I already had so much other required reading for school, you would think that the last thing I would want to do is read. But it became my thing, and I would read right before going to bed. It always had to be filth or nothing too serious or academic. This was my time, so I didn't want to read anything that was going to cause me more stress than I already had.

Lastly, it may not be about removing someone or something from your life, but instead bringing in something new. Maybe you dye your hair a new color, pick up a new hobby, or maybe you rearrange your furniture. When I was a teenager, I would just randomly wake up some days and change my room around. I'm not sure why this was refreshing or made me feel like it was giving me a new perspective, but that's what it did for me. I don't change my room around much these days, but it's not that I don't consider it every once in a while.

Keep Your Support Close

One of my all-time favorite songs is "Nobody Needs Nobody" by Playa Fly. It's a Memphis thang, and if you are ever in my presence and this song comes on just know I'm about to rap every lyric and perform every single time. As much as I love this song, this couldn't be the farthest thing from the truth. Even in the song he says, "All I need is my dogs." But in a sense, he is saying he just needs those who support him around and bump the rest of y'all. The truth is that no one gets through life alone. We all need someone at one point or another.

When I work with clients, one thing we talk about are support systems. When I work with kids, I tell them to think of putting their own superhero team together. Their team should include people they trust. People they can talk to when they are feeling down. People they can tell their true feelings to. We need these things even as adults. I have a best friend that I have been friends with since 1997. She is my person. When it's been a long day at work or a parent almost took me there, she is who I call. By the way I say hello she can instantly tell I'm calling to vent, and it's the same for me when she calls me. Venting isn't going to change your situation, but it does allow you the chance to get it out. We all need someone we can let it all it with without judgment, and someone who is willing to be a support to you but also not being a 'yes friend' or a friend that just tells you what you want to hear. A good friend, or anyone in your support system, should be able to encourage you when needed and tell you about yourself when needed. And you must be open to receive the feedback.

Invest in Yourself

If you don't invest in yourself, who else will? A better question though is if you aren't willing to invest in yourself why should others? When people hear the word invest, the first thing most of us think about is money. Although that is part of it, it's not the only part and honestly may not be the most important part. There are other ways you can invest in yourself. First, you can invest in yourself with knowledge. Whatever you are working towards you can always learn more. No matter how old you are, you should never stop learning.

Reportedly, Albert Einstein said, "Once you stop learning, you start dying." Learning gives you something to look forward to. I laugh when I think about my mom who has a Master's degree and retired from the U.S. Postal Inspection Service because when she retired, she got certified as a nail technician. Always learning. That can be a new skill or furthering your knowledge in your career field.

Another way you can invest in yourself is through your time. How much time are you willing to put into yourself to reach your goals? We can't expect to get further in whatever we are working towards by only putting in minimal time. It's true that you get out what you put in. If you only put a little in, don't be upset when the return on your time investment is very little. One thing I did while working on my dissertation, and what I tell clients when they are working towards something, is to set aside time that you are going to work on that skill or work towards your goal. I knew I would get the most uninterrupted time when working on my dissertation once everybody else was in bed. Therefore, my time to work was after 9pm. I would have my ear buds in, music going, and I would just write, and I would make sure I had at least 2-3 nights that I did this. That didn't mean there weren't other times I wrote but those were my set times that I had to work. Hold yourself accountable to that. Get you an accountability partner if you need it. One thing my sister does that works for her is she color-codes her planner. Blue time may be personal time, time just for her. Green may represent family time. Purple may represent work. Having these set blocks means that she won't schedule anything during those blocks unless it is related to that time block.

Another important aspect of investing in yourself is to take care of yourself mentally, physically, emotionally, and spiritually. One of my favorite therapy quotes is that "You can't pour from an empty cup." Just like I knew I would eventually dry my cup up if I didn't start taking care of myself while my husband was in rehab, we have to do that in our everyday lives. Not just when the shit hits the fan. We have to become more self-aware of our emotions. Take a second and think about the last time you were really stressed. Think about some the physical indicators that may have been there that you didn't pay attention to. Maybe you started to be more fatigued no matter how much sleep you were getting. What about the emotional indicators? Maybe you were easily irritable.

The more self-aware you become, the higher likelihood that you can work to prevent yourself from becoming too stressed and overwhelmed. For example, when we got back from Atlanta, I was home one week before I went back to work. I had been on go and high alert from June 11th until. A lot of people not in education don't realize just how much harder and more stressful the 2021 school year was. Most believed that because we were back in the building that everything was going to be just fine. Let me put in perspective for you. The last time our current 9th graders were in a structured setting was when they were in 7th grade. There is a huge difference between a 7th grader and a 9th grader. Now imagine all of these pseudo-9th graders that are really still at the 7th grade level maturity and behaviorally speaking. Yeah, it was that bad. I told my 9th grade counselor she couldn't pay to come to her hallway. They were off the chain to the COVID-degree. Nah, give me my "Know-it-all" seniors please and thank you.

Beyond the behaviors, the number of students that were behind that year was almost astronomical. Every year I have students behind grade level due to failed classes. I have some classified as 11th, 10th, or even 9th although they should be seniors. On average, I normally have around 40 students that fall in this category. That year I started with over 100 students behind grade level. We had honors and AP students failing. A big part of what I do is work with these students to get them caught up because there is no coming back next year. Once you get your four years, that's it. To say that year was stressful in general is the understatement of the year. Throw in the fact they my year already started stressful due to my husband's illness, and the stress was taking its toll on me. It was to the point that even my school social worker pulled me to the side one day and asked me was I good because my face just looked like I was beyond worn out. And I was. I told him that I was planning on taking a mental health day soon because I could feel how worn and mentally exhausted I was getting. I just had to wait until hubby went back to work because if I was going to take a day and really get a break, I needed a day to just myself. As much as I am an advocate for a healthy work-life balance, working in education is the type of job where it's almost more work for you to take off than to just push through and keep going to work. It's a very unhealthy relationship at times.

Trust Yourself

Sometimes it's harder to put trust in yourself than in others. I'm not talking about trust in the sense of trusting that someone will be faithful to you or honest with you. I'm talking about trusting you and your abilities. When we are working towards our goals, sometimes what is holding us back is that we doubt ourselves and our abilities. In the academic world, you will hear a term called imposter syndrome. Imposter syndrome is that feeling that you have when you feel like you aren't good enough to be in the spaces that you are in. For example, when I received my acceptance letter into my PhD program I second guessed myself a lot. If I'm honest with myself, self-doubt is one the reasons I didn't apply sooner. After I finished my masters, a few people would mention going for the PhD and I would always respond with "I'm gone let this masters marinate." I mean, that was the plan but every time someone said it there would be a small part of me that would think maybe I should. But it would never go much further than a fleeting thought.

Going for a PhD is very intimidating to say the least. Only a fraction of the world holds a PhD. And the mere thought of writing a dissertation. Tuh, I'm good. I mean, what gave me the right to think that I, LaTraci Aldridge, could not only get into a PhD program but also finish it and be called Dr one day? Knowing that others had started but never finished for varying reasons didn't help with my feelings either. So how did to get where I am today?

I stopped doubting myself and had to check in with myself from time to time and remind myself that I'm one dope chick! When I got ready to apply, I didn't tell anybody. I honestly don't remember if I even told my husband before I did it. I had worked on my personal about a year before I even applied. It really started when my grad school boo (Another dope black therapist PhD that I met while working on our Master's) started working on her PhD and told me I had to get my life together and get in a PhD program. I'm pretty sure I told her chile bye, but that really just lit a fire to that small thought of going for it. A big part of it had to do with how we bonded during our Master's and we credit each other for the support that we gave each other through it. So, if my grad school boo could do it, what was stopping me from doing it? Me! That's what!

When the next application season came around, I submitted my application and waited. I still remember the day I received my acceptance letter. I had just come home, and my husband was sitting in the garage with some friends and he says, "Oh you got a letter from Memphis today." I immediately knew what it was and asked for the letter. Y'all this man couldn't remember where he put it. As if my anxiety level wasn't already high, he just pushed it through the roof. Thankfully, it didn't take him too long to find it. Even with the acceptance letter in my hand, there was still the little heffa, imposter syndrome. Did they really mean to send me the acceptance letter?

Anytime you start to feel you don't belong or that you don't deserve to be where you are, you have to think about where you've come from and the accomplishments you have. Those things didn't just happen. It wasn't just chance. It was because you put the work in. You are where you are for a reason. Sometimes we can also get so hung up on society's and others' timelines that we start to doubt ourselves. Something I work on with clients is not focusing on others' timelines. So what someone else had their dream job by 25 and you're 30 still working towards it. We have to realize that what is someone's timeline isn't ours and that isn't a bad thing. In some cases, there are reasons for the assumed delays that we may not see.

For example, I graduated with my Masters in 2010 and immediately went on the job hunt. Since I graduated in December, I wasn't too stressed about not getting a school counselor job in January. However, when it came to May 2011, and I still didn't have a school counselor job that doubt started to sit in. I wasn't hopeless, but I was getting there. Then, I got a job working at a career college as a student counselor in June 2011. I was glad for the job, but it wasn't a school counselor job. It was why I went to school. I knew I was going to be phenomenal school counselor, if someone would just give me chance. I stayed at the career college for two years until I got a job at a virtual K-8 school. One step closer but still not quite there. Yes, it was at a school, but still not in the school counselor role. However, that job ended up being what I needed at the time before I even knew it. My second year on the job, when my oldest started middle school, he was no longer able to ride the bus because we lived too close to the school. That meant he would have to be dropped off and picked up every day. Since my school was virtual, that meant I was at home and could do that. Had I been anywhere else that wouldn't been the case. Not only did it allow me to do that but also became the basis for my dissertation. We never know how a no can be a blessing to us. We just have to trust and believe that what is meant for us is going to be there for us. It may not be on your time, but it will be right on time.

Whatever you are working towards, it is for you. You deserve it. You deserve to be in that space that they told you, you couldn't be in. You deserve everything that you have prayed for, worked for, and waited for. Anybody who tells you different is a hater and someone you need to spring clean out of your life. A few months after my dad died, I was at church, and it was a rough day for me in the grief department. I won't say it was showing, but

I am believer who feels people or things will be shown to you when you need them. After church one of my sorors just felt like she needed to tell me about a conversation she had with my dad before. He was talking about his kids, and he told her that he never really worried about me because he knew I would do whatever I put my mind to. She didn't know how much I needed to hear those words that day. Those words not only helped me that day, but I always refer back to them anytime I feel like I can't do something or if I'm doubting myself or when setbacks come.

You will have setbacks. Everything may not work out exactly how you want it. I've learned that they usually work out how they should. Take those setbacks and use them for setups for the next great thing in your life. You can choose to see setbacks as nothing more than a setback or you can look at them as stepping stones or lessons. When I have a setback, I give myself time to feel that. We are going to have disappointments in life, but that doesn't mean we have to let them become our life. We have to feel them so we can know what it feels like to be on the other side of it. Give yourself time to feel however you feel about the setback, but give yourself a set time limit to do that. It could be an hour or even a day, but once that time is up let it go. Holding on to it will only keep you where you are. It will keep you stuck.

Being stuck can look different for each person. For one person, it can be staying at a job or position because you don't think you can do any better than where you currently are. Or maybe you don't feel you deserve better for yourself. Then there is the self-doubt when you may feel like you don't have what it takes to go to the next level, next position, or next job. Having a certain skillset or education level is only part of what it takes when we are trying to get a better job or higher level in life in general. The other part is having the belief that you can do it and achieve it. Without that, even if you have the skillset, you won't make it far. You may make it in the door, but it won't get you much further than that. It's the motivation and belief in yourself that will get you beyond the door.

How can you get unstuck? First, take a second to think back to previous times when you felt like you couldn't achieve something, but did it. If you were able to do it then, what's different this time? Next, check yourself. Are you putting in the work needed to get where you are trying to go? How many people do you know that swear that nothing is working out for them even though they've been putting in the work? However, you see how they have been working and it's not that much of surprise to you that they are where they are. It's like people who say they want to lose weight but never work out or change their eating habits. I'm just gonna say ouch right here, because I was talking about me there. What about the person who says they want a better job, but will put one application in and then swear no one is hiring? Make it make sense.

If you check yourself and you can't honestly say you are putting in the necessary work, then step your game up and handle your business. Next, put yourself in position. Surround yourself with people who are going places and trying to elevate as well. This is important for several reasons. For one, you need people around you who can uplift and encourage you when times get hard. Additionally, when people are trying to elevate, they want those around them to elevate to. They are accountability partners. You need people who are gonna call you out when you aren't handling our business and will hype you up when you are reaching our milestones. Lastly, sometimes when people aren't elevating nor are they trying to elevate they can't stand to see others elevate. You know those people that rarely or never clap for you or never have time for you but want you to always find time for them. That's your hater, not your uplifter. Know the difference.

I see life as a journey. Most journeys are full of different angles, ups, downs, and some turn arounds. We can choose to look at the dips and lows as obstacles or stepping stones. We can choose to see them as setbacks or opportunities to become better. How we view our lows in life has a high impact on if we persevere through life. One thing I have learned is that you must trust the process. The process is rarely pretty. Trusting the process can be difficult because of the uncertainty of how the journey will end. If we knew for sure how journeys would end when we started that would save us a lot of stress. The things we experience on our journey are only there to help us become the best we can be. I can't speak to why it always feels like one person seems to get everything so easy while for you it seems that you have to always go through something to get to where you want to go, but I can say how you perceive your journey will make a difference. What can you take from your experiences that can help you on your journey? How did those experiences make you better in the long run?

Give Yourself Permission . . .
To Be You and Walk in Your Truth

Falling in love with who you are is one of the most magical things in life. I honestly feel like it's more magical than when you fall in love with your significant other. It's something about looking at yourself or thinking about who you've become and thinking "Damn, girl you got it!" Whatever it is, you got it. Getting to this point is not something that just magically happens one day. It's more of a gradual progress. I can't pinpoint exactly when I came into who I was, but I can think about different points when I started to fall in love with the different parts of me. Oh, cause trust there's levels to me and you, too! Never make yourself one dimensional for anybody.

For as long as I can remember, I have been known as the dancer. In high school, I was the sole black girl on the dance team. One of my assistant principals even coined me as Dancing Queen. Then, when I got to college, I became the light skinned, thick chick on the dance team. If you ask was I popular in high school or college, I will usually respond with no, but most people knew of me. They probably didn't know my name but if you mentioned the girl on the dance team most would be familiar. I am a dancer through and through, even today, but that's only one part of me and most didn't see beyond that. It was almost like they were limiting me to being a dancer and nothing more.

I think we can allow people to put us in boxes and because that's what they expect from us that's what we do regardless of what else we want to do. It's like how we hear and see how some actors are type casted. One that comes to mind is Paula Jai Parker. When you hear her name, what usually comes to mind? Hooker, stripper, addict, etc. She could very well have a deeper range for her acting skills, but will we ever know that or see that on the big screen? Just as the entertainment industry puts people in boxes, our friends, family, or those around us can box us into what they feel we should be. Then, when you come wanting to do something else, they are confused because that's not what you do or who you are. They don't give you the chance show what else there is to you. I'm sure some mean well, but when those closest to you try to keep you in a box it can sometimes help keep you stuck. Because if they don't think you can do it, why should you even try? Not that that is true, but it is what we believe.

As we go through life, we evolve and start to learn more about who we are as individuals. I have always been a pretty confident person, but I can't say I have always known who I am and fully accepted me for me. As my mother will tell you, I am my daddy's child. I'm not afraid to be out in the front and can and will talk to anybody. I'm a very social person and when I really want to, I can talk and then talk some more. However, I know some people who don't care for the talking. Initially, when I felt that someone didn't like that about me, I would just be quiet and not say much. On one end that was okay, but on the other end why should I have to pull myself back because you don't like me? Now what I do is read the room. If I can sense I'm talking too much, I pull back. I try to be intentional on making sure I'm not taking over the conversation. I may miss the mark sometimes, but I do try. When I worked at home, I had to learn this because most days the only person I talked to was me. When I was out, my mind would scream "Oh people!!!" and my mouth would run off. As a social person, not having that daily social interaction would get to me at times.

As social as I am, I have also learned that I am an extroverted introvert. There are days and times that my social meter is tapped out and talking is the last thing I want to do. Some days at work have been nonstop students talking to me with some real issues, and when I would get off the last thing I wanted to do was talk. Then, my husband would call shortly after left work, and I would have minimal conversation for him. He didn't get it. I had to explain to him that some days I'm tapped out and I needed that drive home to decompress not talk.

One thing showed me that I was starting to really know myself and love and accept me was the purchase of a pair of earrings. You may be asking how can some earrings do that? It wasn't so much the earring itself as much as it was the start of finding me. The first pair earrings that started this were some big wooden custom earrings. Before this, I wore earrings, but they were the same earrings you saw on anyone else and always came from a big box store. Nothing special. But these big wooden earrings were just me. I mean, they did have my name on them. That purchase led to another and another. Before I knew it, I had started a collection. And these weren't just any kind of earrings. I have earrings that say "Beautiful by Nature," "Periodt," "Too Much Sauce," and "Black AF." And that just a few of them. What started out as just a regular purchase turned to being an extension of me. Some days the earrings I wear are just because they match the outfit and sometimes they are a representation of my mood or what I'm trying to put into the atmosphere that day. When I took my comprehensive exams for my PhD, I wore a shirt that said, "Not Today Satan" with some earrings that said "Goal Digger." My professor laughed as soon as I walked in. I told him had to set the mood for the day. I didn't have time to play, and I had goals to work on.

Over time, my earrings went from being just accessories to extensions of who I am. They sometimes speak for me without me saying one word. They are more than a fashion statement. They are me. Some days I'm very intentional with what earrings I choose to wear. During Black History Month, I rotate a few different ones: "We Made America Great," "Black AF," "Stolen from Africa," "I am Black History," and "We Out- Harriet Tubman." I have a lot to say and being able to say so much without ever opening my mouth is a great feeling and in ways more powerful than anything I could verbally say. The earrings were just the start of me finding me.

We know for Black women, our hair is also an extension of who we are. Our hair is so versatile, and I love everything about that. I was like most of us who had a relaxer from teenage years through adulthood. However, we started to see more women wearing their hair in its natural state. Honestly, when this started to be more prominent, I wasn't a part of it and wasn't really trying to be. I mean, I saw how my hair did if I sweated a little too much, so I just knew I didn't need it like that on a regular basis. For some, letting go of the relaxer and embracing the natural was almost a spiritual journey or a new beginning. That was not the case for me. What led me to going natural was my friend telling me she couldn't give me a relaxer after taking my braids out. I could've fought her because what was I supposed to do with my hair without a relaxer. She still pressed it out and per usual, it looked great. Since my hair could look like I had a relaxer without having one, I just decided to not get them anymore. That was how my natural journey started, but I still hadn't gotten to the curly phase just yet.

Although I was doing without a relaxer, I had not taken that dive into curly styles. For one, my hair was still in transition with half my hair still having relaxed ends. Then, I honestly was just scared. When everyone around you, including other Black people, make it seem as if straight is the only way you should go that's what you hold on to. Plus, I just wasn't sure what to do with my hair. Eventually, my relaxer grew all the way out and I started thinking about wearing my natural curls. I just had one thing getting in the way of that. That thing was me. Anytime anyone asks about me going natural, I tell them the hardest part is getting over yourself. Once you can get over yourself, you'll just rock your curls fearlessly.

One day I got over myself and started wearing my natural curls, and I haven't looked back. My curls are me, and they are beautiful. I wear my curls unapologetically and the heck with anybody who has a problem with it. A former supervisor found this out one day on one of the rare occasions I straightened my hair. She saw me in the hallway and said, "I like your hair. It looks so professional." I froze in the hallway because I honestly wasn't sure to respond to that. One because she threw me off, and then how do you respond to that? I may not have responded verbally, but I responded with my hair. I went home that night washed my hair and had my curls back the next day. If you know just how much time can go into straightening your hair, you know I really had to feel some time of way. But I did and I wanted to show that I my hair, curly or straight, was professional.

One day I decided to get my hair colored. This wouldn't be my first time getting my hair colored, but it would be my first time going this extreme. Up until that day, anytime I got my hair colored it would be a light brown or a dark blond. You know, the safe colors. But one day I just had a thought to go red. Yep, the first extreme color out the gate I wanted was red. No highlights, but a full head of red hair. I was 100% okay with my decision until I walked past the mirror on the way to the shampoo bowl and saw that I looked like Bozo the clown. Insert cuss words and telling my friend/stylist she was fired for letting me do this. She ensured me she knew what she was doing and that once she did the wash it would not look like that. I'm not a skeptic, but at that moment my skepticism was on 1000%. Thankfully, my friend/stylist was right. After the wash everything was just fine, and I loved my hair. The red was me. I was a red girl with some red hair. And don't let me have a night out because I had to throw on my Ruby woo and have some red lips to go with it too! The red was just another step to finding and loving me.

Since the red, I have had my hair colored a few more times. I have had fuchsia, blue, and a blue and purple mix. It was just something about hair colors that really started to speak to me. My hair color, just like my earrings, became another extension of me. The hair color moved to just as extreme lip sticks. I don't wear makeup often, but just like my hair, I wasn't always into the extreme colors. I still like an overall natural look but a bold lip though! Whew. I have worn red, blue, purple, and green lipstick. And the confidence that comes with wearing a bold lip is something I didn't even know I was missing. I'm confident most days, but it goes up a notch with a bold lip. You can't tell me I'm not dope AF then! I mean, you can, but I wouldn't buy it.

Just like my curls, when it came to hair colors and bold lip colors, I had to get over myself. When I looked in the mirror, the only person whose opinion mattered was mine. No one else's. I didn't think about if someone would like my hair or lip color. I didn't think about if someone wouldn't like it. If I liked it, then I was rocking it. Everybody isn't going to like everything about you. And that's okay. Nobody has to like anything about you. I think we get caught up in thinking that people, including friends and family, have to like everything about us. That's just not the case. That's not to say we shouldn't take into consideration what others, those closest to us, may think. I'm just saying don't let what others think dictate what you do or who you are.

When people struggle to find who they are, a large part of that is because they are so used to doing what others think they should do or they hold back for fear of what others may think. Just like getting the courage rock my natural curls, when you are confidently walking in your truth, you have to get out of your own way and just be you. Take a second, close your eyes if you want, and think about who you are. What is one of your strongest attributes? What are you good at? What makes you the dope individual you are? How often do you do an inventory of your dopeness? I'm not talking about being cocky, but just truly being confident in who are and what makes you who you are. Just as society tells us that wanting me-time is selfish, I think we are also sometimes told to dim our lights, so we don't come off as braggadocious or thinking too highly of ourselves. There is a line between being confident and being cocky. A fine line, but still a line. We have to learn that it's okay to pat ourselves on the back from time to time. You have to be your own hype man. There may not always be a hype man for you. Who better to do that than you?

As I started to embrace more of who I was, I slowly started to notice that I not only like me, but I love me and that I'm pretty dope. A big part of that comes from my perspective on life. I see life as a journey. When you look at life like a journey, you can sit back and see the beauty in the process. A journey is usually filled various sceneries and highs and lows. Life is the same way, but if you don't stop to take a look around along the way you will miss the beauty. While I was in my PhD program, we conducted a marathon group with a group of undergrads. One of the activities was a draw and connect activity. We asked them to draw various items, then had them to draw lines to other people's drawings. Most of them just drew straight lines. However, there was one student who drew loops, curves, and dips. Out of everything on the paper, that is what stuck out to me. I took that as she didn't just like going through life but wanted it to be a journey and to experience things along the way. When I told her this, she thought I had worked some counselor magic on her. It was just me being observant, but it was also how she did that without really thinking.

I'm sure the older we get and the more responsibilities we have, the less we see the journey through life. I'm guilty of this of myself. We wake up, go to work, come home, do dinner, go to sleep and repeat five days a week, day after day. There has to be more to life than just that. And it is, but we have to actively pursue that. When we don't do that, we wake up one day and it's been three years and we can't recall any experiences or the journey we have taken. One thing I ask my clients is are they living just to be living or are they living life. I don't want to look back on my life one day and I say all I did was work and get an education. Those things are great, but they are not what makes life.

When I worked at the career college, I had days I had to work late and there was even period of time when I was the only person in a department, which was Student Services that usually had 4-5 people. To say I was over-worked was an understatement. Not to mention, this became life just a few months after starting the job. Although it was only me, that didn't change the services my department was supposed to provide. But I did it. If I didn't tell you it was just me, you wouldn't have known. I was proud of the work I did there, especially working with students who were working to get their GED. However, all this work cost me in other areas. One day, my oldest, who was around nine or ten at the time, told me that he wished I didn't work at a school because I was always at work. Hearing that was a blow to my stomach.

What do you do with that? It brings to mind the question: Can a working mom really have it all?

I think we can, but there has to be a balance and support. Without these two things, it may not be possible. I won't say it won't be possible, but it may be harder to achieve. Having my son tell me that meant I needed to be more intentional on making sure we got our time together. You may not be able to change your work schedule, but you can make sure you don't bring work home. If you are bringing work home, are you really at home or just working at home? It makes a difference. Weekends were our time. We would go see a movie or go sit down and eat somewhere. There were times we would find activities going on in the city that were different from what we normally did. I can't say that I mastered it, but I can say I'm always trying to get better with it. Now that they are both teens, hanging with momma on the weekend is no longer the highlight of their week, but it doesn't mean I don't still do it to their angst.

When my children are older and think back on life, I want them to be able to say we did this with my mom and dad. My mom took us to these places. We got to go on these trips. We had these different experiences. All of this matters. Even if you aren't able to always finically afford the big the trips, there are so many smaller and local things you can do to give your kids these experiences. It's about the time you are spending with them more than anything else. When I think about my childhood, there are certain things I recall. For example, I think about how we (me, my mom, dad, sister, and brother) would sleep in front of the fireplace as least once during Christmas time. I loved that. My dad would rent a movie and get firewood. Before this exact moment that I'm writing this, I hadn't really thought about why I enjoyed that so much. However, as I was recollecting that memory it reminded why that particular moment may be really special. We did that during Christmas time. My dad died three days before Christmas. Recalling that just now made that memory just that more special. My God, grief is something serious and can hit you when you at least expect it.

Final Thoughts

Well, this book just took me somewhere I wasn't expecting. But that's okay because it still took me where I'm wanting to go through this book. As you go through this journey of finding you, you will learn that one experience, one situation, one mistake doesn't make you who you are. We are more than our mistakes or experiences.

I remember when I got pregnant with my oldest, I had to learn this. I wasn't super young, but I was also not out on my own yet and still in my junior year of college. Prepared for the roll of mother, I was not. One my aunts called me after finding out and she told me, "When you get back home, don't you dare hold your head down. Other people are doing the same thing, they just haven't been found out." That stuck with me. No, I wasn't prepared. Yes, I should have been more careful. However, that didn't mean that should be all I was known for from now on. I took my aunt's advice and didn't hold my head down. I had my moment to feel how I felt and then I picked myself and planned how I would continue working towards my goals while adding my new role of mother.

Because I was so determined to not be considered a statistic or seen as a just another girl who put their child on their parents, I rarely asked for help when I needed it.

I wish I could say I have learned how to 17 years later, but all I can say is that I'm better. When my son was just a few months old, I remember being so tired that I was literally a walking zombie. I was learning my new role while also still continuing my education. One day my mom told me that she would take him for a little while if I needed it. I told her I was fine as I looked at her with half opened eyes. She told me she would give him a bath, and I could rest while she did that. I told her fine but let me know when she finished so I could get him and feed him. Next thing, I knew I was waking up and it was three hours later. Me being me, I went searching for my mom and asked her why she didn't bring him to me. Seventeen years later I hear just how ridiculous that was, but the new mom at the time who was stuck on not being labeled a statistic didn't see that. I don't know how much of this is a pride thing or if it is just the feeling that I know I can take care of it. Even when there are signs I could use some assistance, I'm still reluctant to reach out. I'm a work in progress.

Something else that I have learned along this journey called life is that you have to trust the process. It's something I've said when talking to students, clients, and to my husband during his medical crisis. Trusting the process is one of those many things in life that are easier said than done. I think what makes trusting the process harder in going through my husband's medical crisis is because we didn't know why or how we ended up on this journey. When people are trying to lose weight and they start the work to get healthier and lose weight, they hear trust the process and they can generally tell how they got to this point. Be it years of unhealthy eating, medical issues leading to weight gain, or just lack of exercise and age. The point is we know how we got there.

In this journey my husband and I went through, I couldn't tell you how we got there. One day he was fine and one day he wasn't. We thought maybe his blood pressure was the cause. Nope...tests showed that wasn't case. And also the location of his first stroke showed that wasn't the case. Okay so he has thyroid issues. Maybe that's it. Nope, all tests said his thyroid with his medication had been functioning properly. So, how does a young, relatively healthy male wake up one day to having not just one stroke, but two within a span of a few weeks? In the midst of his recovery, we didn't know why. And months after recovery, we still don't know. And from what multiple doctors we have dealt with have told us, there are about 20% of strokes that they cannot pinpoint why the stroke happened. What do we do with that? How can we prevent this from happening again if we don't even know what caused it? I have no idea. How do we return back to our new normal at some point and I not be worried that at any given moment any little thing could be a trip back to the hospital.......or worse?

The best thing I can do is keep the faith and trust the process. Because if I can't do that, my husband won't be able to. While he was in the hospital, he asked me how could he make this go faster. I had to tell him that there was no fast track to this. He had to trust the process. Not what he wanted to hear, but it's what he needed to hear. Every day he asked for three things multiple times a day. 1. I want to go home 2. I want some food. 3. I want some...yep use your imagination there. Every day! And every day I had to tell him none of those things would be happening because he wasn't there yet. It's hard to sit back and watch someone struggle with not being able to do the things we all do every day without thinking about it.

Imagine going from your everyday life one minute to the next having to learn how to walk again, how to swallow again, how to talk again. That's tough. Even sitting and watching him every day, I couldn't imagine completely what that would be like. But I can tell you that it's hard to be on the other side watching and there is nothing you can physically do about it. I can say that at one point before we went to Atlanta and he kept letting me know he wanted to go home, I was real close to just saying we will find something in Memphis just to help him feel better. But deep down I knew if his doctor recommended a particular facility there was a reason for it and that's where he needed to be. I'm glad I didn't just give in to him wanting to feel more comfortable. Being at Shepherd was the best thing for him. If you were to look at his medical scans during that time, you wouldn't think he could do much more than sitting in the bed. Based on his scans, he should've been in far worse shape than he was in. Oh, but God! Cause this is nothing but God. When doctors can't make sense of it, what else can it be?

Getting to the point of finding you, loving you, and accepting you is an ongoing process of trusting the process. We don't just wake up one day and get to this point. There are even some things we learn about ourselves that we may not like. I'm not talking about that roll of back fat no one likes, but that personality trait that we don't really like. For example, I am an overthinker and over-analyzer. In some cases, this may not be a bad thing. When I'm trying to make a major decision, I will generally think about every possible outcome before I make the decision. That may not seem bad, but if I focus too much or too long on the what-ifs, then I may not get the point of making the decision. On the other hand, overthinking can also be hard when dealing with anxiety and self-depreciating thoughts. When I make a mistake or someone calls me out on something, especially when its work-related, I can sit with it for too long and it puts me in the funk. Sometimes it causes to me to fall back for fearing of messing up again. I had to learn in those situations to give myself time to feel whatever I need to feel then move on from it. Sitting in it wasn't good for me. Sitting in it can also sometimes carry over to other aspects of your life.

While on your journey, you have to speak positivity into yourself, your life, and your journey. When the journey dips low, you have to be able to reach back to those positive affirmations to keep pushing yourself forward. You have to learn when you are getting low and how to recharge yourself. Develop a self-care plan for yourself. These are things you do even when everything seems to be going smoothly. Unfortunately, life likes to throw us curve balls sometimes and when you have an effective self-care plan in place, you can be better prepared to deal with those curve balls. That doesn't mean it won't still knock you to the ground, but you will be in a better position mentally to deal with it.

This is not an all-inclusive self-care plan, but on the next few pages is an outline and it will give you a good starting place to create a self-care plan for yourself. One thing to keep in mind is that your self-care plan is just that. It's yours! What works for you may not work for the next person and what works for others may not work for you.

My Self-Care Plan

Mind

How will you rest your mind? **Ex:** I keep my door closed the 1st 15 minutes of school before classes start to keep my mind at rest. Plan for the day without interruptions.

How will you exercise your mind? **Ex:** I read at night to wind down. Nothing too serious

What are 3 positive affirmations you can tell yourself every day? **Ex:** I am a strong and confident black woman. I can achieve anything I put my mind to.

Body

How will you rest your body? **Ex:** I will go to bed by x:xx time every night. When I don't have any outside of the home activities to do, I will choose times to the use that time to do nothing.

How will you give back to your body? **Ex:** I will walk for 15 minutes at least twice a week

Soul

How will you feed your spirit? **Ex:** Reflect on how you have made progress towards your goals. What did you do good? What can you do better? Meditate. Give back to the community.

Conclusion

I want to thank you for taking this journey with me. I hope something, at least one thing, you read will help you on your journey. If it didn't, well don't tell me. LOL. If nothing else, I hope you enjoyed reading about my journey. Today we are almost two years since my husband suffered a massive stroke. I'm glad to say he is doing much better. He's still recovering some but is able to walk, eat, drive, and get on my nerves. There have been times that I still can't believe what we experienced. I don't ask why. I just sit in awe that we overcame it. I still find myself sometimes looking over to see if he's breathing or even putting my hand on his chest to make sure his chest is moving when he sleeps. Going through something like we did will have you doing things like that. I wouldn't wish this journey on anyone else, but I'm thankful for our journey, nonetheless.

I'm going to leave you with a little gift. My Road to Recovery playlist. Full disclaimer, my playlist is all over the place, and it's not for the faint at heart. It will pull your inner rachet and café days out. It will have you mellowed out wanting to grab some brown liquor with Bobby, then tooting it up with Meg, and then ready to give some loving. But it's me and its who I am. I love her and she is one dope chick!

Road to Recovery Playlist

Divine Legacy
PUBLISHING, LLC.

Creative Control With Self-Publishing

Divine Legacy Publishing provides authors with the guid-ance necessary to take creative control of their work through self-publishing. We provide:

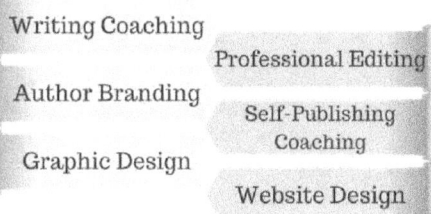

Writing Coaching

Professional Editing

Author Branding

Self-Publishing Coaching

Graphic Design

Website Design

Let Divine Legacy Publishing help you master the business of self-publishing.